After
Journal

Fourth edition printed and bound by Biddles Books Limited
Printed in United Kingdom

First edition printed in United Kingdom, 2018

Text and design by Thought Climber CIC

ISBN 978-1-915787-84-2

This book is dedicated to those facing
the unthinkable loss by suicide. Please
know that you are not alone.

Contents

Welcome --------------------------------- ---------- 8

How to use your After Journal -------- ---------- 9

Practical Matters ---------------------- ---------- 13

Shock, Disbelief, Denial -------------- ---------- 15

Kind To Myself List -------------------- ---------- 30

Postcard To Survivors ----------------- ---------- 31

Anger, Resentment -------------------- ---------- 35

Kind To Myself List -------------------- ---------- 49

Despair, Emptiness, Yearning -------- ---------- 53

Kind To Myself List -------------------- ---------- 68

Postcard To Survivors ----------------- ---------- 69

Recovery, Acceptance, Peace ------- ---------- 73

Kind To Myself List -------------------- ---------- 86

Creative Space ----------------------- ---------- 89

Zoetic Heart Space ------------------- ---------- 102

Personal Thought Drops -------------- ---------- 122

My Milestones ------------------------ ---------- 164

Seasonal Activities ------------------- ---------- 168

Lessons, Insights, and Anything Else -- ---------- 170

My Thank You List -------------------- ---------- 172

Significant Dates --------------------- ---------- 176

Support References ------------------- ---------- 184

The Story Behind The After Journal --- ---------- 188

Welcome

Grief is an instinctive response to any painful loss. Mourning is the inevitable journey that follows. This is how we process the impact of pain and learn new ways to exist in our new reality.

The loss of someone you love is life-transforming and often takes an undefined period of time to heal a profoundly broken heart. While the temptation is to control what we are going through when we cross unchartered waters, no amount of planning or looking ahead can prepare us for a period of mourning. Just take it one day at a time and some days, we might even need to take it one hour at a time.

There is no right or wrong way to face this experience. Every day is different. Some days are easier than others. The entire breadth of our emotions, our physical energy, our ability to do or not do, to be or not be - anything - is alright. We will be alright.

Make a promise to yourself to be patient, especially when it feels like the road you're travelling on is never ending. Be forgiving when you struggle, and give yourself permission to take as long as you need to move forward.

It is often said that no two journeys through grief are the same, just like the shape of snowflakes. The duration of different emotions, how we approach our grief, and how we learn to live with it varies from person to person. However, a common thread that connects each of us is that time brings comfort to our suffering.

My mother always used to say, "Trust the process."

How to use your After Journal
Why keep a journal about your experience?

Writing is a powerful and transformative tool to navigate some of life's most difficult experiences. Our mind can feel overloaded. Our emotions can be all over the place. At these times, writing can help carve a path through the madness.

Every story has invaluabe lessons worth discovering. My hope is for the After Journal to create that safe space for you to reflect, escape, and discover.

Read on for more information about the sections found in this book.

Shock, Disbelief, Numbness, Denial

The sudden nature of suicide can leave you in shock for an extended period of time. It might also be a feeling that comes and goes. There is no "typical" pattern for the different emotions you might experience. But many agree that shock is often the first response to a sudden loss.

Anger, Resentment

This emotion can surface in various ways, if at all.

If we do experience anger, it might be with one's self, with others, with circumstances, or certain ways of thinking in the community. This can be especially true when it comes to a feeling of stigma.

Despair, Emptiness, Yearning

This feeling might not prompt you to write anything at all. You might feel unmotivated which is completely natural.

There is no need to force yourself.

Despair, Emptiness, Yearning

If you experience despair and a lack of motivation then perhaps come back to this section when you feel ready to reflect.

Recovery, Acceptance, Peace

Depending on where you are on your journey, this feeling may seem light years away. This is common, too.

Grief is a journey and recovery is a process that will run its own course. We are not in position to decide this ourselves. However, moments of peace will find their way back into your life. Of this I am certain.

Creativity Space

Sometimes words escape you but there is still a desire to express yourself. Or maybe there is just too much going through your mind and so you are looking for something to help slow down your thought process. Sometimes we just need an activity that helps us to simply breathe and be mindful.

Drawing or colouring can give you that opportunity to capture something without words.

Zoetic Heart Space

Definition of zoetic: ***of or relating to life; living; vital.*** These are the memories we want to keep alive for as long as possible. Fill these hearts with words, collages, or anything else you cherish.

Personal Thought Drops

Think of this as your blank page. Here you can drop solitary thoughts onto the page or carry on thoughts started elsewhere in the journal. Or you can simply paste photos, articles, or just draw. It is entirely up to you how to use this space.

Lessons, Insights, Anything Else

It is important to collect any "pearls of wisdom" gathered along the way.

Significant Dates and References

Significant dates: Certain seasons, weeks, and days hold special significance. Note any of these that mean something to you.

References: These are for social support because this form of grief can feel especially isolating. Please remember that you are not alone.

Why the sprig of boxwood? Its symbolism represents longevity and immortality. It is a gentle reminder that a loved one is forever with us.

"The **reality** is that **you will grieve** forever. You will not 'get over' the loss of a loved one. You will **learn to live** with it. You will **heal** and you will **rebuild yourself** around the loss you have suffered. You will be **whole again** but you will never be the same. Nor should you be the same nor would you want to."
-Elizabeth Kubler-Ross

Practical Matters

Contact details for...

Medical Examiner | GPs:

Funeral Home:

Police | Investigator:

Government & Legal Authorities:

Practical Matters
Work | Hobbies | Social Media | Mobile | School | Inquest | Postal
Service | Friends | Home | Transport | Dentist
Additional Enquiries:

Additional Personal Matters:

SHOCK
DISBELIEF
NUMBNESS
DENIAL

I can recall every single detail about the day you died. Although I carried on with daily tasks and worked through the weeks and months that followed, I don't remember anything about that period. I was just a body going through the motions. On the outside, I saw my reflection in mirrors and windows. But from the inside, I was entirely estranged. I've never felt so lost before. My mind somehow acted on my behalf in any social situation but within my head I was in total darkness. I could look at anything around me and all I felt was emptiness.

I am not entirely sure what I feel. The only way to describe it is...

I cannot believe that you are gone because...

In the aftermath of this loss, people have said many different things to me including...

How do I feel about what they have said?

There are so many things I cannot believe right now. My "I cannot believe" list includes:

I cannot believe

I cannot believe

I cannot believe

I cannot believe

I cannot believe

I cannot believe

I am also feeling overwhelmed by so many unanswered questions. These include:

Are there any activities that are helping me with the shock?
Let me note anything at all that feels `right´ to me.

Who is making this experience more difficult for me? How will I protect my needs at this stage?

Although I am shocked by what happened, am I shocked by the way others respond or treat me?

Do I have certain expectations of others at this stage and am I being realistic?

Do I have certain expectations of myself and am I being realistic?

Am I feeling stuck emotionally, mentally, or physically? If so, how does that make me feel?

Everything I remember about the last time I saw you...

Below, I will list how I can honour my needs during this stage.

Kind To Myself List

A Postcard To Survivors

Below are messages from people who have also lost
a friend or family member to suicide.

If I could express anything it would be...

The compassion you showed
your loved one has only
made their life better.
You could not have done a
better job.

*A message to the
bereaved at this
difficult time*

THOUGHT
CLIMBER

If I could express anything it wou...

It is difficult to express
the immense complexity
of this tragic loss
that more than
anything must leave
on with many
questions to which there
are no answers, save for
gift of their life and love they leave behind.

*A message to the
bereaved at this
difficult time.*

THOUGHT
CLIMBER

A Postcard To Survivors

Below are messages from people who have also lost a friend or family member to suicide.

talk I'm listening.
draw I will observe,
if you need time
I will wait...
If you need tea I will pop the
kettle on ♡

A message to the
bereaved at this
difficult time

I don't know how you
feel or what to say,
but let me know if
you want to talk or
if I can help in
another way.

A message to
the bereaved at
this difficult time

"Life changes fast. Life changes in the instant. You sit down to dinner and life as you know it ends."

– Joan Didion

ANGER
RESENTMENT

I smash dishware, snap furiously, and nobody can grasp my ever-changing moods.

At times, I am incensed by the frivolity of others talking about things like decorating the house, the latest gossip, or any other combination of materialism, egotism, hedonism, extremism, and what have you.

Why am I judging others?

Perhaps it's because I feel that they are judging me when they learn about the suicide. But I didn't choose this. This loss is like a bomb that exploded right in front of me.

So why are they judging me? Why are they isolating me? This only adds to the pain I feel.

At best, their silence makes me feel like an "outsider." At worst, the collective silence of my community isolates me altogether.

Nobody wants to talk about suicide but it's the ONLY thing I really need to talk about.

I am angry about so many things right now and also with certain people. I'm angry with...

When I'm angry I...

Is this how I have always been or am I acting different somehow?

You used to get angry about certain things. How did I feel about it then and how do I feel about it now?

There were times when I felt especially angry with you, like the time when...

Did we forgive each other when we were angry? Does anything remain unresolved? How do I feel about this?

My thoughts continued...

How did we resolve our differences? Is this how I resolve them with others? Is there anything I can learn from this?

There are people and situations that trigger my anger. Who or what are they? What is the healthiest way to manage this?

Do I have expectations of others at this stage? If so, what are they? Are they realistic?

Do I have certain expectations of myself at this stage? If so, what are they? Are they realistic?

If I continue to experience anger and cannot move forward, in what ways can I help myself ?

Is there room for forgiveness? Why or why not? Who should I forgive? Do I need to forgive myself for anything?

Below, I will list how I can honour my needs at this stage.

Kind To Myself List

Space for additional Kind To Myself ideas

"It is the secret of the world that all things subsist and do not die, but retire a little from sight and afterwards return again."

– Ralph Waldo Emerson

DESPAIR
EMPTINESS
YEARNING

I have no energy. I am using what little I have to engage with others, to stay on top of my work, and see a few friends I know I should see... but only for an hour or two at most.

Everything is an enormous chore. I don't even want to get out of bed. My home feels a mess and I don't care. It's not like me. But I don't have the energy to be me, whatever "me" should be at the moment.

Nothing inspires me. Nothing moves me. Everything feels so trivial. Some days all I do is move from the bed to the sofa, then from the sofa to the bed. The only things I want to watch are documentaries about suicide, or addiction, or homelessness, or grief, or any other hardship that communities face.

Human suffering is the only reality I can connect with right now. It makes me feel less alone. Still, even when I am watching that, half the time I just end up falling back asleep.

Emptiness and sorrow can be difficult to define. But it consumes me entirely. How do I describe what this feels like?

I don't really want to do anything I normally like to do. I am uninspired to do things such as...

Am I experiencing grief? Am I experiencing some form of depression? What is the difference?

Does it help me to be alone? Why? Is it possible to be alone too long? How will I know?

Who is especially comforting when I feel down? How do they help me during the difficult moments?

Are there individuals who make me feel worse when I feel down? What's the best way to handle these situations?

My sadness is so widespread because I miss you so much. I miss...

My thoughts continued...

There were still so many things we wanted to do together but now I know we will never...

I have so little energy lately. All I have the energy to do is...

Do I have what I need? How can I improve my self-care?

Am I self-harming? According to the UK National Health Service this means:

cutting or burning self | punching or hitting self | poisoning self with tablets or toxic chemicals | misusing alcohol or drugs | deliberately starving or binge eating | or excessively exercising.

If I continue to experience despair and cannot move forward, how can I help myself?

Below, I'll list out how I can honour my needs during this stage.

Kind To Myself List

A Postcard To Survivors

Below are messages from people who have also lost a friend or family member from suicide.

If I could express anything it would be...

THOUGHT CLIMBER

Many experience this, you are not alone.
Do not be dismayed if people are reticent, it is not necessarily lack of words

A message to the bereaved at this difficult time

lack of concern, but

If I could express anything it would be...

THOUGHT CLIMBER

I would give them a hug but also some space!
I want to be a listening ear and a person to come to
I can't offer a solution but can offer a cup of coffee, maybe a cake and someone to listen ♡

A message to the bereaved at this difficult time

A Postcard To Survivors
Below are messages from people who have also lost a friend or family member from suicide.

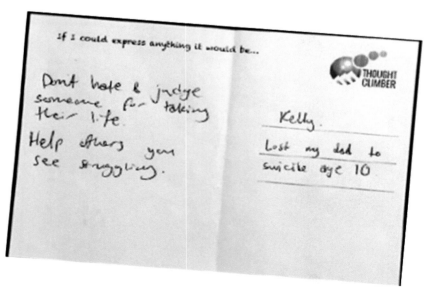

If I could express anything it would be...

There are no words that will make this any better. But I am here for you. If you want to walk, talk, or just sit in silence, we can do any and all of the above. You've got my full support.

A messsage for the bereaved at this difficult time

THOUGHT CLIMBER

If I could express anything it would be...

Dont hate & judge someone for taking their life. Help others you see struggling.

Kelly.

Lost my dad to suicide age 10.

THOUGHT CLIMBER

"New beginnings are often
disguised as painful endings."

– Lao Tzu

RECOVERY
ACCEPTANCE
PEACE

It's true – the days of sadness grow shorter just as the winter nights must give way to the long bright hours of summer.

For so long, it felt like all I could do was survive. I was fighting to keep my head above water both mentally and emotionally. How did I ever get through this?

I don't know quite when it happened but it did. There came a silent yet profoundly spectacular parting of the clouds. The bright glow of life's magic returned miraculously in all its glory, especially when I thought about you. That was the moment I realised that I had survived this unimaginable tragedy.

For the first time in a long time, I realised that I wasn't surviving anymore. Instead, I was finally beginning to thrive once again.

Life without you will never be the same but I recognise now that I am slowly moving forward. I am hoping to...

Since you've been gone, to my surprise, there have been moments when I actually felt happiness. These include:

There are experiences that I know you would want ME to have.
In your honour, I would like to do them. These include...

There were experiences that I know YOU still wanted to have. In your honour, I would like to do them. These include...

It is strange but I feel grateful to be alive. My list of gratitude includes...

Your life taught me many things. Some of the lessons I cherish most and will keep alive are...

One way to keep your spirit alive is through the act of rituals. Below is a list of simple rituals that I would like to commit to...

As I read through other parts of my journal, I now realise how far I have come. Some of the things that surprise me most include...

I know you are with me in spirit. I am happily reminded of you
when...

I have rediscovered joy. Among the things that bring me happiness now are...

More space for happiness and gratitude...

Now that I feel increased strength and joy, I pledge to expand acts of kindness.

Kindness List to Myself and Others

"You are never too old to set another goal or to dream a new dream."

– C.S. Lewis

Creative Space

Art is as natural as sunshine
and as vital as nourishment.
–Mary Ann F. Kohl

Working with colours and creating patterns brings us back to a place where life is much simpler. As children, we had more time to engross ourselves in play. This naturally led to a sense of presence and mindfulness, even though we may have thought of it as something insignificant.

Creativity allows us to reconnect with a part of who we are that is focused and relaxed. It is a space to let our minds journey through its own discovery process.

Use this section to give yourself a break from the traditional forms of "processing" grief through writing and talking. If nothing inspires you, that's alright, too. There are no rules.

"Take care of all your memories, for you cannot relive them."

– Bob Dylan

ZOETIC SPACES

Fill these hearts and the space around them with all the memories you want to hold onto.

ZOETIC SPACES

Memories of your favourite songs, musicians, and genres...

Memories of your favourite expressions and quirky sayings...

ZOETIC SPACES

Memories of your favourite food, dishes, and drinks...

Memories of the different ways you showed me you loved me...

Memories of your favourite ways to celebrate special occasions...

ZOETIC SPACES

Memories of your favourite people and why you loved them...

Memories of the life lessons I have learned from you...

Memories of the qualities I love in you...

Memories of the different things that inspired you...

ZOETIC SPACES

Memories of your favourite places to visit and reasons why...

ZOETIC SPACES

Memories of your favourite literary figures and favourite reading...

More memories that matter to me are...

More memories that matter to me are...

More memories that matter to me are...

More memories that matter to me are...

"Death leaves a heartache no one can heal,
love leaves a memory no one can steal."

– From a headstone in Ireland,
author unknown

The following pages are for my personal "thought drops." These are my musings, images, and anything else I want to drop onto the page.

Thought drop

Thought drop

Thought drop

Thought drop

Thought drop

Thought drop

Thought drop

Thought drop

Thought drop

Thought drop

Thought drop

Thought drop

Thought drop

Thought drop

Thought drop

Thought drop

Thought drop

Thought drop

Thought drop

Thought drop

Thought drop

Thought drop

Thought drop

Thought drop

Thought drop

Thought drop

Thought drop

Thought drop

Thought drop

Thought drop

Thought drop

Thought drop

Thought drop

Thought drop

Thought drop

Thought drop

Thought drop

Thought drop

Thought drop

Thought drop

Thought drop

Tragedy can stop time. It can feel like life is moving forward while I remain stuck. To remember that I am moving forward, I will keep a list of small milestones. These include the small efforts – like getting up, cleaning, or taking a walk – to bigger things like taking on a new challenge, new job, or a life changing habit.

My milestones

My milestones

My milestones

My milestones

For the days I feel uninspired but might still benefit from doing something, here are just a few ideas.

In spring I will:
- plant something in your honour
- visit a region that is especially beautiful in spring
- note the longer days and how I might spend them
- spot any spring flowers beginning to appear

In summer I will:
- find somewhere to swim or enjoy the sea, lake, or river
- find a peaceful spot to either dine or sit outdoors
- observe the sounds and fragrances of summer
- take a long walk somewhere you liked to visit

In autumn I will:
- observe leaves changing colour
- pick autumn produce from a local farm
- observe flowers and plants in the local landscape
- slowly breathe in the autumn air

In winter I will:
- make a winter donation in your honour
- take a morning walk in the crisp winter air
- enjoy your favourite winter activity
- collect fallen pinecones and decorate them in your favourite ~rs

Other seasonal activities that come to mind are...

Lessons learned, new insights and ideas, and anything else worth holding onto...

Lessons learned, new insights and ideas, and anything else
worth holding onto...

I cannot forget to acknowledge those who helped me along the way.

My Thank You List

My Thank You List

"The time is ripe for looking back over the day, the week, the year, and trying to figure out where we have come from and where we are going to for sifting through the things we have done and the things we have left undone for a clue to who we are and who, for better or worse, we are becoming. But again and again we avoid the long thoughts. We cling to the present out of wariness of the past. And why not, after all? We get confused. We need such escape as we can find. But there is a deeper need yet, I think, and that is the need—not all the time, surely, but from time to time—to enter that still room within us all where the past lives on as a part of the present, where the dead are alive again, where we are most alive ourselves to turnings and to where our journeys have brought us. The name of the room is Remember—the room where with patience, with charity, with quietness of heart, we remember consciously to remember the lives we have lived."

-Frederick Buechner
A Room Called Remember: Uncollected Pieces

Significant Dates

Month _____

Month _____

Month _____

Significant Dates

Month _____

Month _____

Month _____

Significant Dates

Month _____

Month _____

Month _____

Significant Dates

Month _____

Month _____

Month _____

Additional notes, dates, and holidays

Notes, dates, and holidays

References - U.K.

SOBS | Survivors of Bereavement by Suicide
Helpline: 0300 111 5065 | Monday and Tuesday 9:00 – 17:00
www.uksobs.org

Support After Suicide
www.supportaftersuicide.org.uk
Help Is At Hand, **free download** at:
https://supportaftersuicide.org.uk/resource/help-is-at-hand/

B.A.G.S. for Strife
www.bagsforstrife.co.uk

Suicide Bereavement UK
www.suicidebereavementuk.com

Cruse Bereavement Care
Helpline: 0808 808 1677 | Monday to Friday 9:30-17:00, Saturday
and Sunday 10:00 – 14:00
www.cruse.org.uk

Papyrus
Helpline: 0800 068 4141 | Open 24 hours a day
SMS: 0786 003 9967
www.papyrus-uk.org

Winston's Wish
Helpline: 08088 020 021 | Monday to Friday 08:00-20:00
www.winstonswish.org

References – U.K.

Child Bereavement UK

Helpline: 0800 02 888 40

Live chat via website

www.childbereavementuk.org

Coroners' Court Support Service

Helpline: 0300 111 2141

www.coronerscourtssupportservice.org.uk

Samaritans

Helpline: 116 123 | Every day, 24 hours

www.samaritans.org

References – International

AFSP | American Foundation for Suicide Prevention

www.afsp.org

Skylight | New Zealand

www.skylight.org.nz

Standby Support After Suicide

Helpline: 1 300 727247

www.standbysupport.com.au

IASP | International Association for Suicide Prevention

www.iasp.info

SAVE | Suicide Awareness Voices of Education

Resources for Survivors of Suicide

www.save.org

My own support references

My own support references

The Story Behind The AFTER JOURNAL

On November 17, 2014, I lost the single most influential person in my life: my mother. Her death was sudden and tragic because it was the result of suicide.

To know her was to love her. She possessed a seemingly unwavering passion for life and exuded joy and generosity at every level. Her death changed everything instantly.

For many months, I felt like time stood still while everyone around me continued to move forward. Any sense of progression felt alien to me and I soon felt like life was leaving me behind. I lost my direction and didn't understand what I was supposed to do and who I was supposed to be. I felt frozen in time, completely disorientated and unable to establish a sense of purpose or clear identity.

Life lost its meaning for many months thereafter and although I didn't want to die, I couldn't understand how I was supposed to live either. The nature of life itself was flipped entirely upside down. All that I once knew to be true no longer held the same credibility. I didn't believe in it anymore.

So, I retreated into a world of blank pages as they have always been like a trusted old friend. These pages protect my messily scribbled thoughts, vulnerabilities and an ongoing series of unanswered questions.

I journalled relentlessly. At first, there were so many thoughts travelling through my mind, so many new experiences I couldn't

understand. I filled the pages day after day. In a "stream of consciousness" style, I recorded everything from the cyclone like emotions to the silent stagnation in my own mental activity.

After a few months I hit the proverbial wall of writer's block. Nothing new surfaced. There were no new thoughts, only the same cycle of difficult emotions. As a result, I began to write the same thought over and over again: I'm stuck. I'm stuck in time. I'm stuck mentally. I'm stuck emotionally. When I don't have to be at work, I'm even stuck inside my home.

So, I began to obsessively research the psychological impact of suicide, of crisis and mental health, and the aftermath of trauma. In other words, I soaked up any relevant information I could get my hands on and that might help me understand what I was going through.

By the spring of 2015, my former partner and I rescued a beautiful Siberian husky named Thunder. Thunder and I would go for long walks in the woods in Reigate Priory Park in Surrey. The natural landscape and spring flowers brought immense comfort at a time when I might have otherwise just remained in bed.

The beauty of the colours and textures inspired me to revisit a decade of my own floral photography and floral design work while once in the industry. Slowly, new ideas began to emerge about death and life; about ugliness and beauty; about suffering and healing; and about the various paths we all take to reach a single, universal place of refuge: a place of deeper understanding

Pulling together all that I had learned, I began to design the sort of bereavement journal I wish I had at the onset of my loss. When the blank pages began to intimidate and frustrate me and "grief journals" felt too prescriptive and limiting for what I was trying to understand, the After Journal subsequently came to life. I believed that a combination of both a blank journal and a grief journal that included practical information and writing prompts would help to navigate the uncertainty of this traumatic stress.

The journey following suicide is incredibly overwhelming and isolating at times. However, please have faith that time ultimately brings you to a more stable and life-affirming place. I, along with countless others, are living proof that we each have the capacity to survive, thrive, and continue. For me, writing was the pathway that enabled my safe journey from crisis to healing.

Let the written words of your own story reveal all the wisdom that will carry you through.

With love.